MW01594825

# THE BODY Teaches MANY LESSONS

written by
S. C. Ashour & Véronique M.P. Chevrier

illustrated by
Stephen Marchesi

## Level 1
### BOOK 1

**TOBET** THEOLOGY OF THE BODY
EVANGELIZATION TEAM

Dedicated to the Church, including our family and friends,
and especially to Mother Mary and Saint John Paul.

Tremendous thanks to all TOBET members over the years.
Special thanks to Andrea, Jacques, Jean, Joseph, Kathy, Lizzy, Rose, Sheryl, and Theresa.

We are grateful for consultation work by the translator of the Theology of the Body,
Dr. Michael Waldstein, as well as Dr. Susan Waldstein and Dr. Danielle M. Peters.

*Nihil Obstat:*  Tomas Fuerte, S.T.L.
*Censor Librorum*

*Imprimatur:*  +Most Reverend Samuel J. Aquila, S.T.L.
Archbishop of Denver
Denver, Colorado, USA
July 26, 2018

Library of Congress information on file. ISBN 978-1-945845-10-9 • Second Printing, 2019
Cover Design: FigDesign  •  Layout: Emily Gudde  •  Editor: Dayspring Brock  •  Associate Editor: Alexis Mausolf

Based on *Man and Woman He Created Them: A Theology of the Body* translated by Michael Waldstein, Copyright © 2006. Used by permission of Pauline Books & Media, 50 Saint Paul's Ave, Boston, Massachusetts 02130. All rights reserved. www.pauline.org.

# Table of Contents

# 1 The Body Teaches

There are many ways to learn about human beings. One way is by looking at what their bodies teach.

4

Luke and Matt see the
zookeeper standing in
the alligator pen.

Does that mean they
think the zookeeper
is an alligator?

No! He is human!
His body teaches this.

5

Everyone can see that John is pretending to be a dinosaur.

Even though he looks like a dinosaur, of course he is still human!

His body teaches this.

Everyone can see that people come from different parts of the world. Whether Asian or African, Anglo or Latin (or any other heritage), everybody is human.

Their bodies teach this.

Everyone can see that Kim is young and her grandpa is elderly.

Whether young or old, everybody is human.

Their bodies teach this.

Everyone can see that some human bodies are bigger, and others are smaller.

No matter what size or shape, everybody is human.

Their bodies teach this.

Everyone can see that Paz
and her cousin are girls.

Their bodies teach this.

Everyone can see that
John and Pierre are boys.

Their bodies teach this.

Whether boy or girl,
everybody is human.

Everyone can see that some people have special needs. Whatever special needs people have, everybody is human.

Their bodies teach this.

The body teaches that all people are different, yet everyBODY is still human.

What else does the human body teach?

## 2 The Body Teaches About Humans

Even though people are different,
they all share common experiences.
The body can show this.

Can you think of experiences that
all humans share?

Mia's body teaches that she is cold from swimming in the lake. She shivers and wraps herself in a towel.

Everybody feels cold sometimes.

That's part of being human.

Pierre's body teaches that he is growing up. He lost a baby tooth.

Everybody loses baby teeth.

That's part of being human.

Paz's body teaches that she is hungry. She holds her stomach while it growls.

Everybody feels hunger sometimes.

That's part of being human.

John's body teaches that he lost his balance. He slipped on the ice while trying to turn.

Everybody makes mistakes sometimes.

That's part of being human.

Mia's body teaches that she created a new hairstyle. She looks in the mirror and smiles.

Everybody is creative sometimes.

That's part of being human.

Dee's body teaches that she likes to move to the music. She sways her arms to the beat.

Everybody has fun sometimes.

That's part of being human.

Luke's body teaches that his arm hurts. His dad takes him to the doctor.

Everybody hurts sometimes.

That's part of being human.

Ben's body teaches that he can't wait to play outside. He's ready to jump and run.

Everybody gets excited sometimes.

That's part of being human.

God designed EveryBODY to
share common experiences.

Isn't it great to have a human body?

# 3 Humans Can Choose to Wait

One common experience that the human body can teach is that all people have needs like food, water, and shelter.

But when people wait to meet their needs because of something more important, they show self-control.

They wait for the **right time**, in the **right place**, to do the **right thing**, in the **right way**.

Look how these children can learn self-control.

Shawn's body teaches him that his feet are wet. But the middle of the soccer game is not the **right time** to dry off.

Shawn chooses self-control to help his team and waits to dry off later.

John's body teaches him that he is hungry. But church is not the **right place** to eat a snack.

John chooses self-control because he is old enough to eat later, out of respect for God and others.

Ben's body teaches that he has a bad cold. He still wants to play with his friends. But playing with friends is not the **right thing** to do when he is sick.

Ben chooses self-control by staying home so his friends don't get sick.

Ruth's body teaches her that she needs to go to the bathroom. Others have the same need. But cutting in line is not the **right way** to act.

Ruth chooses self-control by waiting in line to be kind to others.

Paz's body teaches her that she needs to concentrate. Silence is for concentration. But since her little sister is crying, it is not the **right time** to concentrate.

Paz chooses self-control by caring for her sister.

Kim's body teaches her that she is sleepy. Rest is for sleepiness. But music class is not the **right place** to sleep.

Kim chooses self-control to stay awake and learn with all the others.

Baby Clare is too little to choose self-control when she wants cookies. Mia chooses the **right way** to help her by playing with a puppet.

Baby Clare will soon learn self-control like her big sister.

It is good to grow up and learn self-control. By waiting for the **right time**, in the **right place**, to do the **right thing**, in the **right way**, everyBODY can live well together!

 The Body Teaches People to Care

An important lesson the human body teaches is that people are meant to care for each other.

When he was little, Pierre's body taught his mom that he needed help.

Pierre's mom cared for him by helping him reach his letters.

Ruth's body teaches her dad that she needs help as she learns to pedal.

Ruth's dad cares for her by steadying her bike.

Dee's body teaches her friends that she needs people to play with her carefully.

Dee's friends care for her by throwing a beach ball so she can easily catch it.

Shawn's body teaches his family that he is excited to blow out his candles.

Shawn's family cares for him by singing "Happy Birthday."

Kim's body teaches her sister that she is sad to have lost her kitten.

Kim's sister cares for her by giving her a hug.

Shawn's body teaches
Ruth that he is upset.

Ruth cares for him by
feeling sad with him and
then cheering him up.

At the school play, Mrs. Jacob's body teaches John that she is elderly and needs a seat.

John cares for her by giving her his chair.

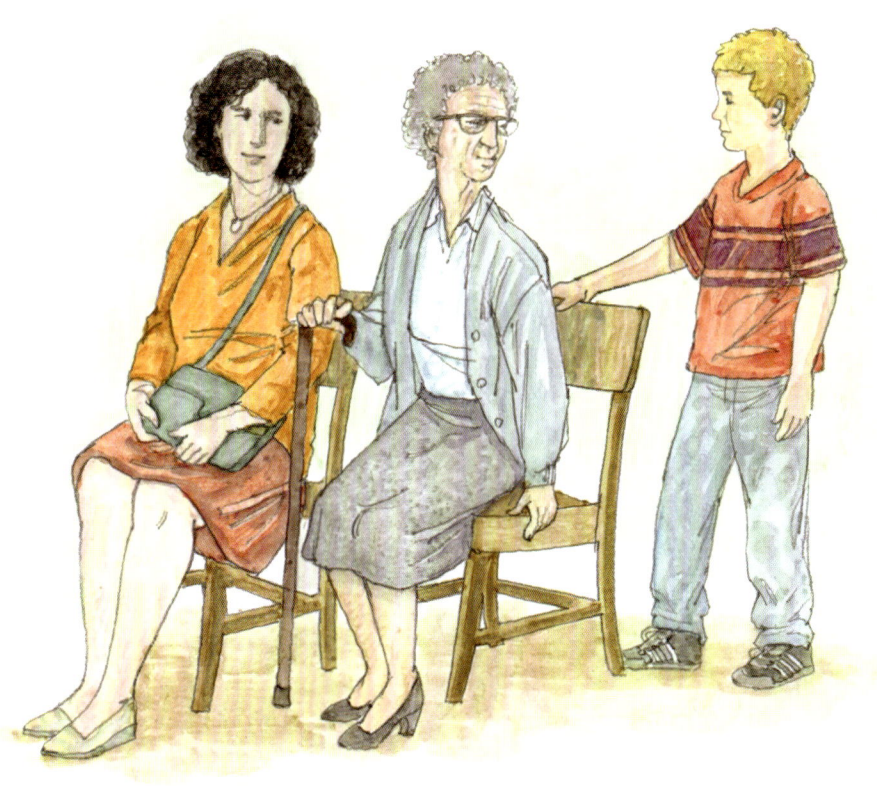

At the art gallery, this man's body teaches the need for silence.

Ben cares for him by being quiet.

Sister Jane Karol's body teaches that she is praying.

Paz cares for her by praying for her and all the sisters.

Jesus' Body on the cross teaches that He loves everyone so much that He gives His very life for them.

By laying down his life, He cares for the world and forgives people's sins.

Jesus' Resurrected Body teaches that He is more powerful than death.

He cares for people by offering them this power. They are now able to live with Him forever.

Father Jim's body
teaches that Jesus
is here at Mass.

When lifting up the
Body of Christ, the
priest shows that
Jesus is present
and cares for all.

Mother Mary's body teaches Jesus that she cares for Him.

As Mother of the Savior, she cares for everyone else too. She shows us how to come to Jesus with our needs.

EveryBODY can see that humans are meant to care for each other.

Isn't it amazing how much the body teaches?

How wonderful are the works of the Lord and how wonderfully made is the human body!